# Just for Today

Ruth Cherry, Ph.D.

Ginny Conrow

Lewis Andrei

Inks and Bindings
888-290-5218
www.inksandbindings.com
orders@inksandbindings.com

*Ruth Cherry, Ph.D., Ginny Conrow and Lewis Andrei*

*In our Yes we find peace.*

*Meditation is life cut small.*

*At my core I am one with Source.*

*I watch my feelings move through me and
I don't identify with them.*

*Our essence is Source.*

*Meditation allows us to experience WHAT IS.*

*Release one old resentment today.*

Today, forgive yourself and everyone else.

*Be still for five minutes. Let your breath carry your attention into your eternal center.*

*Today, practice non-resistance.*

*Today, speak honestly from your heart.*

*The patterns in our significant relationships reflect the way we treat ourselves*

*Everything is a lesson.*

We need to discard distracting overlays that tell
us we are not good enough.

*To trust in and surrender to life
is our sacred task.*

*Today, accept whatever crosses your path.*

*If there isn't anything we can do to make life
turn out as we want, we need to go inside,
practice stillness and pay attention.*

*It's the quality of our attention that lends
sacredness to the moment.*

*WHAT IS isn't the problem, it's how we interpret it that is.*

*Healing happens when we feel our feelings, look at our beliefs and keep breathing.*

*The process of transformation is about practicing availability.*

22

*Today, notice your critical thoughts.*

*Today, trust your intuition.*

*Integrating your vulnerability lights
your soul's way home.*

25

*You practice presence when you watch yourself without judgement as you move through day.*

*Being a good parent to yourself means being aware of your needs, your feelings and your patterns of resistance.*

*How does your resistance to your inner world*
*affect your aliveness?*

*Today, notice that a Wisdom greater than your intellect's lives in you.*

*Live today with passion, saying YES to whatever is in front of you.*

*Today, practice respect for your unique being.*

*Ruth Cherry, Ph.D., Ginny Conrow and Lewis Andrei*

*Today, acknowledge your feelings without identifying with your feelings.*

Today, practice humility. Say Thank You
for whatever happens.

*Today, let inspiration guide your decisions.*

*When you operate at the level of peace,
there are no problems, only opportunities.*

*Freedom starts inside.*

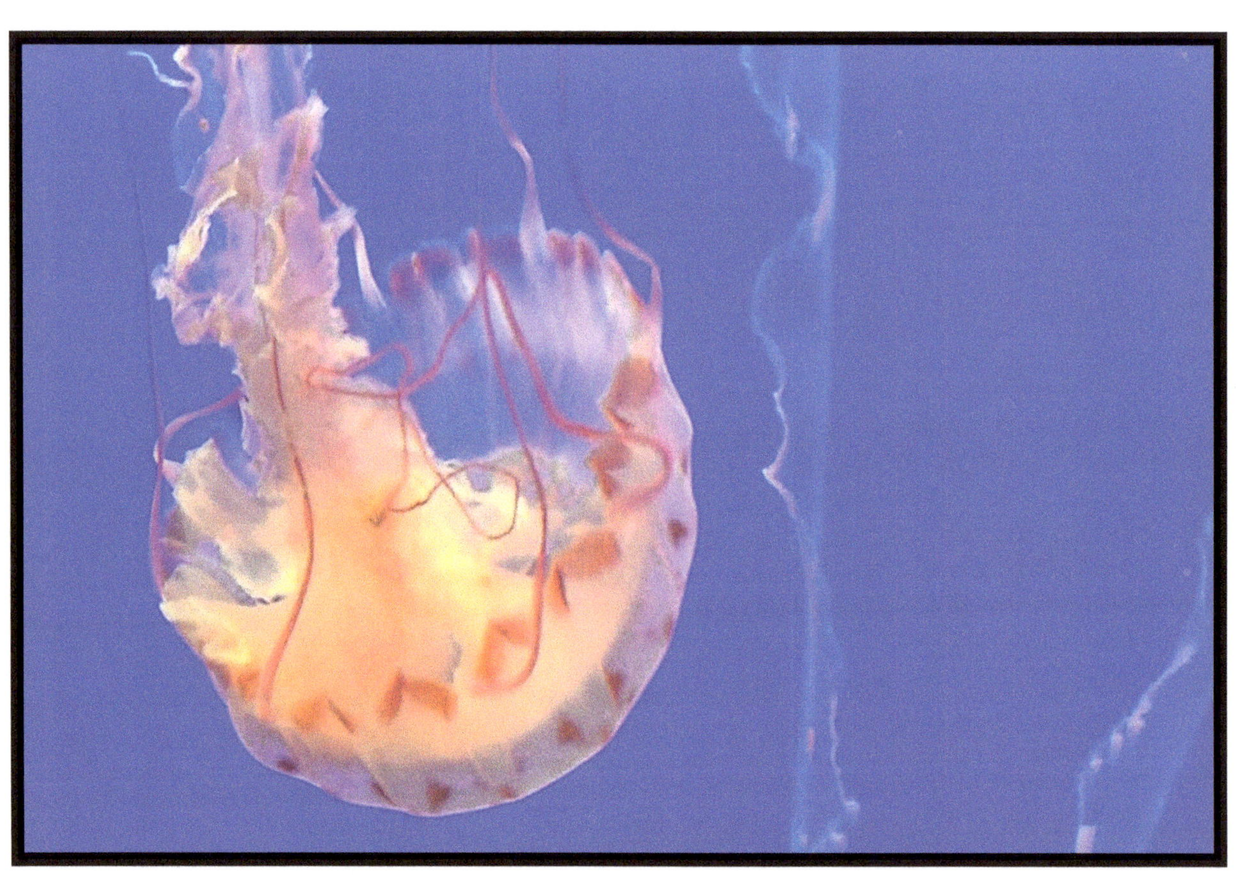

*Healing requires surrender.*

*Being grateful helps me stay open to receive.*

*When we live from the peace at our center,*
*we cooperate with Life in the*
*ever-creative flow of being.*

*Today, move beyond judgment and thinking to noticing and allowing.*

*Today, I look at my fear and accept it.*

*We don't judge anything inside us when we practice surrender. Just for today, practice not judging anything inside or outside you.*

*We are vibrational beings, so in every second change is possible.*

*Acknowledging your own spiritual reality
responds to your heart's longing.*

Reality is larger than your intellect.

*Today, I spend time alone in silence.*

*Today, notice how life responds to your availability.*

*If we don't experience emotional balance
and self-acceptance, we distort
our spirituality clarity.*

*What I react to in others is a projection of what goes on inside me.*

When we have a relationship with own fear we
are willing to know it and to feel
it and to look at it.

*Let yourself want something you can't effect on your own.*

*Today, I notice my Victim thoughts.*

Today, replace control with sensitive observation.

*Be an Observer and notice the themes and subtleties in your life.*

*The unconscious is our connection to spiritual reality.*

*When you think about trusting the ongoing flow of life inside and outside you, what scares you?*

For 20 minutes today make a commitment to be available to your inner world.

*Identify with your Observer and watch
yourself move through today.*

*Your Spiritual Warrior doesn't accept
mediocrity from you.*

At the level of peace you are asked to let go.

*We can't choose to participate in external reality
with any meaningful depth while avoiding our
own inner reality.*

*Today, invite magic to work in your life.*

*Discontent is a sign that you're being invited to express more of your soul consciousness.*

*Ruth Cherry, Ph.D., Ginny Conrow and Lewis Andrei*

*Play with nature today and notice how nature plays with you.*

*Imagine giant garden shears cutting any
unnecessary ties to the past.*

*Today, trust that your healing proceeds even though your intellect may not understand it.*

*Watch your thoughts and feelings as they move through you.*

*Wherever I am, Source is.*

*Today, practice not reacting to conditions around you. Stay anchored in your eternal center no matter what happens.*

*Today, I choose to experience my oneness with
Source and I release anything in me
that inhibits that.*

*When we say "I want to honor my heart's longings," we open to transformation.*

*Today, practice gratitude for what is in your life
that you don't want.*

*The purpose of any kind of mask is to shield our inner world vulnerability.*

*We discover the Spiritual Warrior within us when we confront our vulnerability and feel the pain and confusion and uncertainty that lives within us.*

*Reality is. What we are willing to know of reality determines what we experience.*

*A simple spiritual prescription for a successful life: release resentment and let your light shine.*

# Today, choose the vibration you want
to practice.

*Being carries us where doing can't.*

*Today, ask the Universe for help
in a specific situation.*

*Today, practice presence and allow.*

*Every day and every second Source beckons to us.*